The Che[illegible]
Bib[illegible]

Cheesecake Recipes for Every Day

Indulgent

BY

Carla Hale

License Notes

Table of Contents

Introduction

My love for cheesecake evolved after I tried cheesecake for the very first time on a family cruise vacation. I will never forget the day that I tried that piece of cheesecake. I was intrigued by the flavor of cheesecake and excited to try something so exotic. The very first bite I took melted in my mouth and suddenly a whole new world of dessert possibilities opened before me. Even then, I had tried a plain slice of cheesecake, but I began to wonder what it would have tasted like if cherry flavor was added or if it had been topped off with cookies. And thus, my journey to making cheesecake began.

The journey has been a rough one and I have made plenty of mistakes along the way. However, throughout that journey my love of cheesecake has only grown, and I am so excited to teach you everything I have discovered in the world of cheesecake. By the end of this cheesecake cookbook, it is my hope that you will learn from my mistakes and learn how to make most cheesecake recipes with ease.

So, let's stop wasting time and get to baking some cheesecake!

Nutty Cheesecake Bars

This is one of the most popular and easy cheesecake recipes you can make to satisfy mouths of all ages. It is great for your next family gathering.

Makes: 16 to 20 servings

Total Prep Time: 1 hour and 40 minutes

Ingredients for the cheesecake:

- 2 cups of all-purpose flour
- 1 cup of walnuts, chopped
- 2/3 cup of light brown sugar
- ½ tsp. of salt
- 2/3 cup of butter, cold and cut into pieces

Ingredients for the filling:

- 2, 8 ounce packs of cream cheese, soft
- ½ cup of white sugar
- 2 eggs, beaten
- ¼ cup of whole milk
- 1 tsp. of pure vanilla

Directions:

1. In a bowl, add in the all-purpose flour, chopped walnuts, light brown sugar and salt. Add in the butter and cut in with a pastry cutter until crumbly in consistency. Set half of this mix aside. Add half of the crumb mix into the bottom of a greased baking dish. Press down firmly.

2. Place into the oven to bake for 10 to 15 minutes at 350 degrees or until light brown.

3. In a separate bowl, add in the soft cream cheese, white sugar, eggs, whole milk and pure vanilla. Beat with an electric mixer until smooth in consistency. Pour over the baked crust.

4. Sprinkle the remaining crumb mixture over the top.

5. Place into the oven to bake for 20 to 25 minutes at 350 degrees or until baked through.

6. Remove and set aside to cool for 1 hour.

7. Slice into bars and serve.

Sugar Cookie Cheesecake

This is a sweet tasting cheesecake you can make whenever you have a craving for something sweet. It is great tasting and perfect to make during the Christmas holidays.

Makes: 12 servings

Total Prep Time: 4 hours and 10 minutes

Ingredients for the base:

- ½ cup of butter, soft
- ½ cup of white sugar
- 1 egg
- 1 tsp. of pure vanilla
- 1 tsp. of baker's style baking soda
- 1 tsp. of salt
- 1 ¼ cup of all-purpose flour
- ¼ cup of rainbow sprinkles

Ingredients for the cheesecake:

- 4, 8 ounce carton cream cheese, soft
- 1 cup of white sugar
- 2 tsp. of pure vanilla
- 4 eggs

Ingredients for the whipped topping:

- ½ cup of heavy whipping cream
- 1 ½ Tbsp. of powdered sugar
- 2 Tbsp. of rainbow sprinkles
- Sugar cookies, for decorating

Directions:

1. Preheat the oven to 325 degrees.

2. Prepare the crust. Grease a 9 inch springform pan with cooking spray. In a bowl, add in the butter and white sugar. Beat with an electric mixer until fluffy in consistency. Add in the egg and pure vanilla. Continue to beat until smooth in consistency. Add in the dash of salt and baker's style baking soda. Beat well to incorporate.

3. Add in the all-purpose flour and beat well to ix. Add in the rainbow sprinkles and fold gently to incorporate.

4. Press the crust mix into the baking dish.

5. Prepare the filling. In a separate bowl, add in the cream cheese and white sugar. Beat with an electric mixer until smooth in consistency. Add in the pure vanilla and egg. Continue to beat until mixed. Pour over the crust.

6. Place into the oven to bake for 1 hour or until the center is set. Remove and set aside to cool.

7. Cover and set into the fridge to chill for 4 hours.

8. Prepare the topping. In a chilled bowl, add in the heavy whipping cream and powdered sugar. Beat with an electric mixer until a stiff peaks start to form on the surface. Add in the rainbow sprinkles and then continue to beat until mixed.

9. Spread the topping over the top of the cheesecake. Garnish with the sugar cookies.

10. Slice and serve.

Oreo Cheesecake Pie

This Oreo cheesecake is so easy to make, you can have it ready in just a matter of minutes. Even though it is simple to put together, it does not lack in flavor.

Makes: 8 servings

Total Prep Time: 1 hour and 5 minutes

Ingredients:

- 1, 24.3 ounce container of readymade cheesecake filling
- 1 ½ cups of Oreos, crushed and evenly divided
- 1,9 inch chocolate crumb crust

Directions:

1. In a bowl, add in the container of cheesecake filling and 1 ¼ cups of the crushed Oreos. Stir well to evenly mix.

2. Pour into the chocolate crumb crust.

3. Sprinkle the remaining crushed Oreos over the top.

4. Cover and set into the fridge to chill for 1 hour.

5. Serve.

Lime and Coconut Cheesecake

This is a refreshing cheesecake that is made with a perfectly crunch coconut crust. It is easy to make and perfect for practically any occasion.

Makes: 10 to 12 servings

Total Prep Time: 5 hours and 30 minutes

Ingredients:

- 1 ½ cups of sweetened coconut, shredded
- 3 Tbsp. of powdered macadamia nuts
- 3 Tbsp. of butter, melted
- 1 envelope of unflavored gelatin
- ¼ cup of cold water
- ¾ cup of white sugar
- 2, 8 ounce packs of cream cheese, soft
- ¼ cup of lime juice
- 1 Tbsp. of lime zest
- 3 drops of green food coloring
- 1 ½ cups of heavy whipping cream
- Toasted coconut, for garnish
- Whipped cream, for topping

Directions:

1. In a bowl, add in the shredded coconut and ground macadamia nuts. Add in the melted butter. Stir well to mix. Press this mix into the bottom of a 9 inch springform pan.

2. Place into the oven to bake for 10 to 15 minutes at 350 degrees or until golden brown. Remove and set aside to cool.

3. In a saucepan add in the cold water and gelatin. Allow to rest for 1 minute. Add in the white sugar. Cook over low heat until dissolved. Remove from heat.

4. In a separate bowl, add in the cream cheese. Beat with an electric mixer until smooth in consistency. Add in the gelatin mix and beat until evenly mixed. Add in the lime juice, green food coloring, lime zest and whipped cream. Beat well to incorporate.

5. Pour over the crust.

6. Cover and place into the fridge to chill for 5 hours.

7. Remove the cheesecake from the springform pan.

8. Serve with a garnish of toasted coconut and whipped cream.

Caramel Apple Cheesecake

This is the perfect cheesecake dish for you to make during the fall season. In terms of preparation, it is pretty straightforward.

Makes: 8 servings

Total Prep Time: 11 hours and 30 minutes

Ingredients for the crust:

- 1 cup of gingersnap cookie crumbs
- ½ cup of pecans, toasted and chopped
- ¼ cup of butter, melted
- 2 Tbsp. of light brown sugar

Ingredients for the filling:

- 2, 8 ounce packs of cream cheese, soft
- ¾ cup of light brown sugar
- 1 egg
- ¼ tsp. of apple pie spice

Ingredients for the topping:

- 3 pounds of tart apples, peeled and sliced into wedges
- 1/3 cup of light brown sugar
- 1 Tbsp. of butter
- 2 Tbsp. of apple jelly

Directions:

1. Preheat the oven to 375 degrees.

2. Prepare the crust. In a bowl, add in the cookie crumbs, chopped pecans, melted butter and light brown sugar. Stir well to mix. Press into the bottom of a 9 inch springform.

3. Prepare the filling. In a bowl, add in the cream cheese, light brown sugar, egg and apple pie spice. Beat with an electric mixer until smooth in consistency. Pour into the crust.

4. Place the springform pan onto a baking sheet.

5. Place into the oven to bake for 20 to 25 minutes or until the center is set. Remove and set aside to cool completely. Cover and set into the fridge to chill for 8 hours.

6. Prepare the topping. In a bowl, add in the light brown sugar and apple wedges. Stir well to mix. In a skillet set over medium to high heat, add in 1 tablespoon of butter. Once melted, add in the apple mix. Cook for 15 to 18 minutes or until golden brown. Remove and set aside to cool for 30 minutes.

7. Place the apples over the cheesecake to decorate. Brush the apples with half of the apple jelly.

8. Preheat the oven to broil. Place the cheesecake into the oven. Broil for 2 to 3 minutes or until the apples begin to turn brown. Remove and brush with the remaining apple jelly.

9. Cover and place into the fridge to chill for 1 hour.

10. Serve.

Banana Cream Cheesecake

This is a lovely cheesecake dessert you can make whenever you are expecting company. It is the perfect finale to any meal that you may make.

Makes: 10 servings

Total Prep Time: 1 to 2 hours and 25 minutes

Ingredients for the crust:

- 1 ¾ cups of graham cracker crumbs
- ¼ cup of white sugar
- ½ cup of butter, melted

Ingredients for the filling:

- 1, 8 ounce pack of cream cheese, soft
- ½ cup of white sugar
- 1, 8 ounce carton of whipped topping, evenly divided
- 3 to 4 bananas, thinly sliced
- 1 ¾ cup of cold milk
- 1, 3.4 ounce pack of instant banana cream pudding mix

Directions:

1. In a bowl, add in the graham cracker crumbs and white sugar. Add in the ½ cup of butter and stir well to mix. Set aside ½ cup of the mix. Press the remaining mix into the bottom of a greased 9 inch springform pan.

2. Place into the oven to bake for 5 to 8 minutes at 350 degrees. Remove and set aside to cool completely.

3. In a bowl, add in the cream cheese and ½ cup of white sugar. Beat with an electric mixer until smooth in consistency. Add in 2 cups of the whipped topping and fold gently to incorporate.

4. Add half of the banana slices on top of the crust. Top off with half of the whipped topping. Repeat these layers once more.

5. In a separate bowl, add in the whole milk and instant pudding mix. Whisk to mix. Allow to rest for 2 minutes. Add in the remaining whipped topping and fold gently to mix. Pour over the cheese layer.

6. Sprinkle the remaining crumb mixture over the top.

7. Cover and place into the fridge to chill for 1 to 2 hours or until set.

8. Serve.

Funfetti Cheesecake

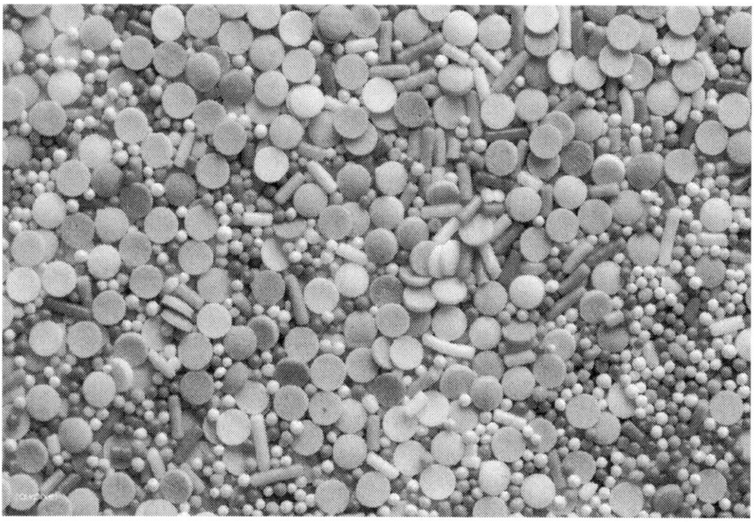

This is the perfect cheesecake recipe for you to make for your next birthday bash. This cheesecake is made using cake mix, to make a delicious treat everybody will love.

Makes: 10 servings

Total Prep Time: 7 hours

Ingredients:

- 1 box of Funfetti cake mix + ingredients listed on the box
- 3, 8 ounce packs of cream cheese, soft
- 1 cup of white sugar
- 3 eggs
- ¼ cup of sour cream
- 2 tsp. of pure vanilla
- ½ cup of rainbow sprinkles, extra for decorating
- ½ cup of vanilla frosting

Directions:

1. Preheat the oven to 350 degrees. Grease a 9 inch springform pan with cooking spray.

2. Prepare the box of funfetti cake mix according to the directions on the package. Pour half of the batter into the springform pan. Place into the oven to bake for 25 minutes or until baked through. Remove and set aside to cool completely.

3. In a bowl, add in the cream cheese and white sugar. Beat with an electric mixer until smooth in consistency. Add in the eggs, sour cream and pure vanilla. Continue to beat until mixed. Add in the rainbow sprinkles. Fold gently to incorporate.

4. Pour the batter over the cooled cake mix.

5. Place into the oven to bake for 1 hour and 10 minutes. Remove and set aside to cool completely. Cover and place into the fridge to chill for 4 hours.

6. Pipe the frosting on top of the cheesecake.

7. Garnish with the extra rainbow sprinkles.

8. Slice and serve.

Peanut Butter and Cheese Cheesecake

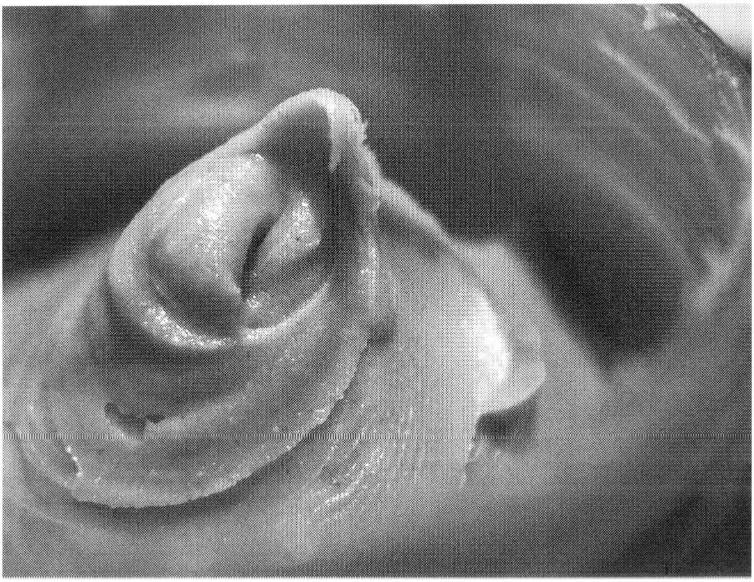

This dessert dish has been a favorite in my home and once your own family gets a taste of it, it will soon become a favorite in your home.

Makes: 14 to 16 servings

Total Prep Time: 7 hours and 20 minutes

Ingredients for the crust:

- 1 cup of graham cracker crumbs
- ¼ cup of light brown sugar
- ¼ cup of butter, melted
- ½ cup of peanuts, chopped

Ingredients for the filling:

- 2 cups of creamy peanut butter
- 2, 8 ounce packs of cream cheese, soft
- 2 cups of white sugar
- 2 Tbsp. of butter, soft
- 2 tsp. of pure vanilla
- 1 ½ cups of heavy whipping cream

Ingredients for the topping:

- 4 ounces of semisweet chocolate chips
- 3 Tbsp. + 2 tsp. of brewed coffee
- Peanuts, chopped

Directions:

1. Prepare the crust. In a bowl, add in the graham cracker crumbs, butter, light brown sugar and chopped peanuts. Stir well to mix. Press the crust mix into the bottom of a 10 inch springform pan. Cover and set into the fridge to chill.

2. In a separate bowl, add in the creamy peanut butter, soft cream cheese, white sugar, butter and pure vanilla. Beat with a highest setting for 2 minutes or until smooth in consistency. Add in the heavy whipping cream. Fold gently to incorporate.

3. Pour the filling over the crust.

4. Cover and set into the fridge to chill for 6 hours.

5. Prepare the topping. In a bowl, add in the chocolate chips and coffee. Allow to rest until melted. Whisk until smooth in consistency. Spread over the top of the cheesecake filling.

6. Cover and set into the fridge to chill for 30 minutes or until firm.

7. Garnish with the chopped peanuts and serve.

Red Velvet Cheesecake

This is a delicious cheesecake recipe that contains the rich flavor of red velvet cake and the fluffiness of a cheesecake that I know you will love.

Makes: 8 servings

Total Prep Time: 3 hours and 50 minutes

Ingredients:

- 2, 8 ounce packs of cream cheese, soft
- ½ cup of white sugar
- 1 tsp. of pure vanilla
- 2 eggs
- 2 ounces of semisweet chocolate, melted
- 1 Tbsp. of red food coloring
- 1, 6 ounce chocolate crumb crust

Directions:

1. Preheat the oven to 350 degrees.

2. In a bowl, add in the cream cheese, white sugar and pure vanilla. Beat with an electric mixer until evenly mixed. Add in the eggs and continue to beat until mixed.

3. Add 1 cup of the batter into a bowl. Add in the melted semisweet chocolate and red food coloring. Stir well to mix.

4. Pour into the chocolate crumb crust. Top off with the remaining filling.

5. Place into the oven to bake for 40 minutes or until set.

6. Remove and set aside to cool completely. Cover and place into the fridge to chill for 3 hours.

7. Serve.

Pina Colada Cheesecake

Make this cheesecake whenever you want to feel like you are taking a trip to the tropics. Made with pineapple and a little rum, this is a cheesecake that is packed with a Caribbean flavor.

Makes: 8 servings

Total Prep Time: 9 hours and 20 minutes

Ingredients:

- 6 Tbsp. of butter, melted
- 1 ¾ cups of graham cracker crumbs
- ¾ cup of pecans, toasted and chopped
- 1 Tbsp. of white sugar
- 3, 8 ounce packs of cream cheese, soft
- ½ cup of white sugar
- 5 eggs
- 1, 8 ounce can of pineapple, crushed
- 1 cup of cream of coconut
- 1 cup of sour cream
- 1/3 cup of light rum
- 4 tsp. of coconut extract
- Whipped cream, for garnish
- Coconut, toasted and for garnish

Ingredients for the glaze:

- 1 Tbsp. of cornstarch
- 1 Tbsp. of water
- 1, 8 ounce can of pineapple, crushed
- ¼ cup of white sugar
- 2 Tbsp. of lemon juice

Directions:

1. Preheat the oven to 325 degrees. Grease a 9 inch springform pan.

2. In a bowl, add in the melted butter, graham cracker crumbs, toasted pecans and white sugar. Stir well to mix. Press into the greased springform pan.

3. In a separate bowl, add in the soft cream cheese and ½ cup of white sugar. Beat with an electric mixer until fluffy in consistency. Add in the eggs, crushed pineapple, coconut cream, sour cream, rum and coconut extract. Continue to beat until mixed.

4. Pour the filling over the crust in the springform pan.

5. Place into the oven to bake for 1 hour and 15 minutes or until the cheesecake is set. Remove and set aside to cool completely.

6. In a bowl, add in the cornstarch and 1 tablespoon of water. Whisk until smooth in consistency.

7. In a saucepan set over medium heat, add in the crushed pineapple, ¼ cup of white sugar and lemon juice. Add in the cornstarch mix. Stir well to mix. Cook for 5 minutes or until thick in consistency. Remove and set aside to cool completely.

8. Spread the glaze over the top of the cheesecake.

9. Cover and set into the fridge to chill for 8 hours.

10. Slice and serve.

Triple Chocolate Cheesecake

This is a cheesecake recipe that every chocolate lover will fall in love with. Best of all, it is used with only a few ingredients, making it perfect for those who have never made cheesecake before.

Makes: 12 servings

Total Prep Time: 1 hour and 40 minutes

Ingredients for the crust:

- 24 Oreo cookies, crushed
- ¼ cup of butter, melted

Ingredients for the filling:

- 2 pounds of cream cheese, soft
- 1 ½ cups of powdered sugar
- 3 Tbsp. of powdered cocoa
- 4 eggs
- 10 ounces of bittersweet chocolate, chopped

Ingredients for the topping:

- ¾ cup of heavy whipping cream
- 6 ounces of bittersweet chocolate, chopped
- 1 Tbsp. of white sugar

Directions:

1. In a bowl, add in 350 degrees. Grease a 9 inch springform pan.

2. In a food processor, add in the Oreo cookies and melted butter. Pulse until moist. Press into the bottom of the springform pan.

3. Place the crust into the oven to bake for 7 minutes. Remove and set aside to cool completely.

4. Prepare the filling. In a bowl, add in the 10 ounces of chocolate. Microwave for 1 minute or until melted. Add in the cream cheese, white sugar, powdered cocoa and eggs. Beat with an electric mixer until smooth in consistency.

5. Pour into the crust.

6. Place into the oven to bake for 1 hour or until the top is set. Remove and set aside to cool completely. Cover and set into the fridge to chill for 8 hours.

7. Prepare the topping. In a saucepan set over low heat, add in the heavy whipping cream, chopped chocolate and white sugar. Stir well until melted. Remove from heat and set aside to cool for 10 minutes. Pour over the cheesecake.

8. Garnish with chocolate curls and serve.

Cinnamon Roll Cheesecake

If you love the taste of cinnamon rolls, then this is one cheesecake dish I know you are going to especially love.

Makes: 9 servings

Total Prep Time: 2 hours and 10 minutes

Ingredients for the crust:

- 1 ½ cups of Nilla wafer crumbs
- 4 Tbsp. of white sugar
- 1 tsp. of powdered cinnamon
- 5 Tbsp. of butter

Ingredients for the cheesecake:

- 3, 8 ounce packs of cream cheese, soft
- 1 cup of white sugar
- 3 Tbsp. of all-purpose flour
- 4 eggs
- 1 cup of sour cream
- 2 tsp. of pure vanilla
- 2 tsp. of powdered cinnamon

Ingredients for the filling:

- 2 cups of light brown sugar
- 5 Tbsp. of powdered cinnamon
- ¾ cup of all-purpose flour
- 12 Tbsp. of butter, melted

Ingredients for the icing:

- 2 Tbsp. of cream cheese
- 6 Tbsp. of butter, soft
- ½ tsp. of pure vanilla
- 1 ½ cups of powdered sugar
- 4 to 5 Tbsp. of whole milk

Directions:

1. Preheat the oven to 325 degrees.

2. Prepare the crust. In a bowl, add in the Nilla wafer crumbs, white sugar, powdered cinnamon and butter. Stir well until evenly mixed. Press into the bottom of a 9 inch springform pan. Place into the oven to bake for 10 minutes. Remove and set aside to cool.

3. Wrap the outside of the springform pan with aluminum foil. Set aside.

4. Lower the temperature of the oven to 300 degrees.

5. Prepare the filling and cheesecake. In a bowl, add in the cream cheese, white sugar and all-purpose flour. Stir well until mixed. Add in the eggs, sour cream, pure vanilla and powdered cinnamon. Beat with an electric mixer on the lowest setting until mixed. Set aside.

6. In a separate bowl, add in the light brown sugar, powdered cinnamon, melted butter and all-purpose flour. Whisk well until mixed. Sprinkle over the bottom of the crust.

7. Spread 1/3 of the filling over the crumble mix. Repeat these layers until the cheesecake and the filling have been used. Sprinkle the remaining cinnamon mix over the top.

8. Place the springform pan into a roasting pan. Fill the outside of the springform pan with water halfway.

9. Place into the oven to bake for 1 hour and 20 minutes. Turn off the oven. Allow the cheesecake to rest in the oven for 30 minutes. Open the door slightly and continue to rest for 5 minutes. Remove and set aside to cool completely. Cover and set into the fridge to chill completely.

10. Prepare the icing. In a bowl, add in the cream cheese, soft butter, pure vanilla, whole milk and powdered sugar. Beat with an electric mixer until smooth in consistency. Spread over the top of the cheesecake.

11. Slice and serve.

Classic Strawberry Cheesecake

This is one of the most classic cheesecake recipes you will ever find. It is a simple cheesecake that you can make regardless of the occasion.

Makes: 12 servings

Total Prep Time: 6 hours and 30 minutes

Ingredients for the cheesecake:

- 3, 8 ounce packs of cream cheese, soft
- 1 cup of white sugar
- 3 eggs
- ¼ cup of sour cream
- 1 tsp. of pure vanilla
- 1 tsp. of lemon zest
- Strawberries, thinly sliced and for garnish

Ingredients for the crust:

- 15 graham crackers, crushed
- 5 Tbsp. of butter, melted
- 2 Tbsp. of white sugar
- Dash of salt

Ingredients for the sauce:

- 1 cup of strawberry preserves
- 2 tsp. of lemon juice

Directions:

1. Preheat the oven to 325 degrees. Grease a 9 inch springform pan with cooking spray.

2. Prepare the cheesecake. In a bowl, add in the cream cheese and white sugar. Beat with an electric mixer until smooth in consistency. Add in the eggs, sour cream, pure vanilla and lemon zest. Continue to beat until mixed.

3. Prepare the crust. In a bowl, add in the graham cracker crumbs, white sugar, melted butter and salt. Stir well to mix. Press into the bottom of the springform pan. Pour the cheesecake mix over the top of the crust.

4. Place into the oven to bake for 1 hour and 10 minutes or until the center is set. Turn off the oven. Allow the cheesecake to cool for 1 hour in the oven.

5. Cover and place into the fridge to chill for 4 hours.

6. Prepare the glaze. In a saucepan set over medium heat, add in the strawberry preserves and lemon juice. Whisk until smooth in consistency. Allow to come to a simmer. Remove from heat and set aside to cool.

7. Place the strawberries over the top of the cheesecake. Brush the glaze over the strawberries.

8. Cover and set back into the fridge to chill for 1 hour.

9. Slice and serve.

Pumpkin Cheesecake Bars

These sweet and creamy cheesecake bars are perfect to have whenever you have a strong sweet tooth that needs to be satisfied.

Makes: 9 servings

Total Prep Time: 50 minutes

Ingredients for the crust:

- ¾ cup of crushed chocolate graham crackers
- 4 Tbsp. of butter, melted

Ingredients for the filling:

- 2, 8 ounce packs of cream cheese, soft
- 1 cup of white sugar
- ¾ cup of pureed pumpkin
- 2 tsp. of pure vanilla
- 3 Tbsp. of all-purpose flour
- 1 ½ tsp. of pumpkin spice
- ¼ tsp. of salt
- 2 eggs, beaten

Directions:

1. Preheat the oven to 350 degrees. In a baking dish, add in a sheet of parchment paper.

2. Prepare the crust. In a food processor, add in the chocolate graham crackers and melted butter. Pulse until mixed. Press into the bottom of the baking dish. Place into the oven to bake for 8 minutes. Remove and set aside.

3. Prepare the filling. In a bowl, add in the cream cheese. Beat with an electric mixer for 30 seconds or until creamy in consistency. Add in the white sugar, pureed pumpkin, pure vanilla, all-purpose flour, pumpkin spice, salt and beaten eggs. Continue to beat until mixed.

4. Pour the filling over the crust.

5. Place into the oven to bake for 35 to 38 minutes. Remove and set aside to cool completely. Cover and place into the fridge to chill for 2 to 4 hours.

6. Slice and serve.

Reese's Cheesecake

This is the perfect cheesecake to make for every peanut butter lover in your home. Made with plenty of Reese's pieces, this is a cheesecake dish everybody in your family won't be able to get enough of.

Makes: 12 servings

Total Prep Time: 7 hours and 25 minutes

Ingredients for the crust:

- 20 Nutter butters
- 6 Tbsp. of butter, melted

Ingredients for the cheesecake:

- 22 Reese’s peanut butter cups, evenly divided
- 3, 8 ounce packs of cream cheese, soft
- ¾ cup of white sugar
- 3 eggs
- 1 cup of cream peanut butter, evenly divided
- ¼ cup of sour cream
- 1 tsp. of pure vanilla
- Reese’s pieces, for topping

Directions:

1. Preheat the oven to 350 degrees. Wrap a 9 inch springform pan in two sheets of aluminum foil.

2. Prepare the crust. In a food processor, add in the nutter butters and melted butter. Pulse well until mixed. Press this mix into the bottom of the springform pan.

3. Add a layer of 16 Reese's cups over the top of the crust.

4. Prepare the filling. In a bowl, add in the cream cheese and white sugar. Beat with an electric mixer until smooth in consistency. Add in the eggs, ¾ cup of the creamy peanut butter, sour cream and pure vanilla. Continue to beat until mixed. Pour over the Reese's cups in the pan.

5. Place the springform pan into a roasting pan filled with 2 inches of water.

6. Place into the oven to bake for 1 hour. Turn off the oven and open the door. Allow the cheesecake to rest for 1 hour. Cover and place into the fridge to chill for 5 hours.

7. Drizzle the remaining peanut butter over the cheesecake. Decorate with the remaining Reese’s cups and Reese’s pieces.

8. Slice and serve.

Caramel Cheesecake Bars

Make these delicious cheesecake bars right in time for the Halloween holiday season. It is so delicious, I guarantee your guests will be begging you for the recipe.

Makes: 15 servings

Total Prep Time: 50 minutes

Ingredients for the crust:

- 2 ¼ cups of ground graham crackers
- 2 Tbsp. of white sugar
- ¼ tsp. of powdered cinnamon
- 10 Tbsp. of butter, melted

Ingredients for the filling:

- 3, 8 ounce packs of cream cheese
- 1 cup of white sugar
- 3 eggs
- ½ cup of dulce de leche
- 2 tsp. of pure vanilla

Ingredients for the caramel topping:

- 2/3 cup of dulce de leche
- 2 to 3 Tbsp. of heavy whipping cream
- 2 to 3 Tbsp. of caramel sauce

Directions:

1. Preheat the oven to 350 degrees. Grease a baking dish with cooking spray.

2. Prepare the crust. In a bowl, add in the ground graham crackers, white sugar, powdered cinnamon and melted butter. Stir well to mix. Press into the bottom of the baking dish. Place into the oven to bake for 10 minutes or until golden. Remove and set aside to cool completely.

3. Prepare the filling. In a separate bowl, add in the cream cheese, white sugar, eggs, dulce de leche and pure vanilla. Beat with an electric mixer until smooth in consistency. Pour over the crust in the baking dish.

4. Place into the oven to bake for 35 minutes or until set. Remove and cool completely.

5. Prepare the topping. In a bowl, add in the dulce de leche, heavy whipping cream and caramel sauce. Beat with an electric mixer until smooth in consistency.

6. Pour the caramel sauce over the bars.

7. Slice and serve.

Eggnog Cheesecake

This is the perfect cheesecake for you to make just in time for the Christmas holiday season. Made with a gingersnap crust, it is a cheesecake dish the entire family will be begging for seconds for.

Makes: 12 servings

Total Prep Time: 9 hours and 10 minutes

Ingredients:

- 12 ounces of gingersnaps, ground
- ¼ cup of white sugar
- ¼ cup of melted butter
- 32 ounces of low fat cream cheese
- 4 eggs
- 2 cups of eggnog, evenly divided
- 2 cups of powdered sugar
- 2 Tbsp. of all-purpose flour
- 1 cup of heavy whipping cream
- Grated nutmeg, for garnish

Directions:

1. In a bowl, add in the ground gingersnaps, white sugar and melted butter. Stir well to mix. Press into the bottom of a 10 inch springform pan.

2. in a bowl, add in the cream cheese. Beat with an electric mixer until smooth in consistency. Add in the eggs, 1 ½ cups of eggnog, powdered sugar and all-purpose flour. Continue to beat until smooth. Pour over the crust in the pan.

3. Place into the oven to bake for 1 hour at 325 degrees. Turn off the oven. Allow the cheesecake to rest in the oven for 1 hour. Cover and place into the fridge to chill for 8 hours.

4. In a bowl, add in the heavy whipping cream. Beat with an electric mixer until peaks begin to form on the surface. Add in the remaining ½ cup of eggnog. Fold to gently incorporate.

5. Spread over the top of the cheesecake.

6. Slice and serve.

Lemon Bar Cheesecake

This is a delicious cheesecake dish that is packed full of a fresh lemony flavor that nobody will be able to resist. Feel free to indulge yourself in this dish whenever you need something sweet.

Makes: 10 to 12 servings

Total Prep Time: 22 hours and 45 minutes

Ingredients:

- 2 cups of all-purpose flour
- ½ cup of powdered sugar
- ¼ tsp. of salt
- ½ cup of butter, cold and cut into cubes
- 2 egg yolks
- 1 to 2 Tbsp. of ice water
- 4, 8 ounce packs of cream cheese, soft
- 1 cup of white sugar
- 4 eggs
- 2 tsp. of pure vanilla
- 2 cups of lemon curd, evenly divided
- Candied lemon slices, for garnish

Directions:

1. In a food processor, add in the all-purpose flour, powdered sugar and dash of salt. Pulse until evenly blended. Add in the cold butter and continue to pulse until crumbly in consistency.

2. Add in the egg yolks and ice water. Continue to pulse until mixed.

3. Wrap the dough in a sheet of plastic wrap. Cover and set into the fridge to chill for 4 hours.

4. Roll the dough into a 14 inch sized circle on a flat surface. Place into a 9 inch springform pan. Cover and place into the fridge to chill for 30 minutes.

5. Preheat the oven to 325 degrees.

6. In a bowl, add in the cream cheese, 1 cup of white sugar, eggs and pure vanilla. Beat with an electric mixer until smooth in consistency.

7. Pour 2/3 of the filling over the crust. Add 1 cup of the lemon curd. Swirl around with a knife. Pour the remaining filling over the top.

8. Place into the oven to bake for 1 hour and 10 minutes or until the center is set. Remove from the oven and set aside to cool completely. Cover and chill for 8 hours.

9. Spoon remaining cup of lemon curd over the cheesecake.

10. Top off with the candied lemon slices. Slice and serve.

Tiramisu Cheesecake

This is the perfect cheesecake dish for you to make for those incredibly special occasions that you need to celebrate.

Makes: 8 to 10 servings

Total Prep Time: 8 hours

Ingredients for the crust:

- 1 sleeve of graham crackers, crushed
- 5 Tbsp. of butter, melted
- ¼ cup of white sugar
- 1 Tbsp. of powdered cocoa

Ingredients for the cheesecake:

- 4, 8 ounce bars of cream cheese, soft
- 1 ½ cup of white sugar
- ¼ cup of cornstarch
- 4 eggs
- 1/3 cup of rum
- 1/3 cup of brewed espresso
- 1 tsp. of pure vanilla
- 12 lady fingers

Ingredients for serving:

- 2 cups of whipped topping
- ¼ cup of powdered cocoa, for dusting
- 2 Tbsp. of chocolate shavings

Directions:

1. Preheat the oven to 325 degrees. Grease a 9 inch springform pan with cooking spray.

2. Prepare the crust. In a bowl, add in the crushed graham crackers, melted butter, white sugar and powdered cocoa. Stir well to mix. Press into the bottom of the springform pan.

3. Prepare the filling. In a bowl, add in the bars of cream cheese and white sugar. Beat with an electric mixer until smooth in consistency. Add in the cornstarch, eggs, rum, brewed espresso and pure vanilla. Continue to beat until fluffy in consistency.

4. Pour half of the batter into the springform pan. Add a layer of the ladyfingers. Top off with the remaining batter.

5. Place into the oven to bake for 1 hour and 20 minutes. Turn off the oven. Allow the cheesecake to rest in the oven for an additional hour. Cover and place into the fridge to chill for 4 hours.

6. Dust the top of the cheesecake with powdered cocoa, dollops of the whipped topping and chocolate shavings.

Chocolate Truffle Cheesecake

This is an elegant cheesecake that is perfect to make just in time for the holiday season. It is so delicious, nobody will be able to say no to a slice.

Makes: 10 servings

Total Prep Time: 12 hours and 25 minutes

Ingredients:

- 1 ½ cups of dark chocolate and almond shortbread cookies
- 2 Tbsp. of butter, melted
- 2, 4 ounce semisweet chocolate bars, chopped
- 1 cup of heavy whipping cream
- 4, 8 ounce packs of cream cheese, soft
- 1, 14 ounce can of sweet condensed milk
- 2 tsp. of pure vanilla
- 4 eggs
- Raspberries, for garnish

Ingredients for the ganache:

- 1 cup of heavy whipping cream
- 1, 4 ounce semisweet chocolate
- 1, 4 ounce dark chocolate bar

Directions:

1. Preheat the oven to 300 degrees.

2. In a bowl, add the cookies and the melted butter. Crush well until fine in consistency. Press into the bottom of a 9 inch springform pan.

3. In a separate bowl, add the semisweet chocolate bars and 1 cup of heavy whipping cream. Microwave for 1 minute or until melted. Stir well until smooth in consistency.

4. In a separate bowl, add in the 2, 4 ounce packs of cream cheese. Beat with an electric mixer until smooth in consistency. Add in the can of condensed milk, eggs, pure vanilla and chocolate mix. Continue to beat until smooth in consistency.

5. Pour the batter over the crust in the springform pan.

6. Place into the oven to bake for 1 hour and 5 minutes or until the center is set. Turn off the oven. Allow to rest inside the oven for 30 minutes. Remove and cool completely. Cover and set into the fridge to chill for 8 hours.

7. Remove the cheesecake from the pan.

8. Prepare the ganache. In a saucepan set over medium heat, add in the heavy whipping cream. Allow to come to a simmer. Remove from heat.

9. In a food processor, add in the semisweet and dark chocolate. While the food processor is running, pour in the simmering heavy whipping cream. Continue to pulse until smooth in consistency. Allow to cool for 20 minutes.

10. Pour the ganache over the cheesecake.

11. Cover and place back into the fridge to chill for 1 hour before serving.

Chocolate and Espresso Cheesecake

Espresso and chocolate help to make a decadent cheese that is so delicious, you will want to spoil yourself with it as often as possible.

Makes: 12 servings

Total Prep Time: 10 hours and 25 minutes

Ingredients for the crust:

- 1 cup of chocolate wafer cookies
- 1 Tbsp. of white sugar
- 4 Tbsp. of butter, melted

Ingredients for the filling:

- 4 tsp. of powdered instant espresso, evenly divided
- 3, 8 ounce packs of cream cheese
- 1 1/3 cups + 3 Tbsp. of white sugar
- 4 eggs
- 2 ½ cups of sour cream
- 3 Tbsp. of all-purpose flour
- 4 ounces of unsweetened chocolate
- Powdered cocoa, for garnish

Directions:

1. In a roasting pan filled with 2 inches of water, set into the bottom rack of your oven. Preheat the oven to 325 degrees. Cover a springform pan with a sheet of aluminum foil. Grease with cooking spray.

2. In a bowl, add in the chocolate wafer cookies, white sugar and melted butter. Stir well to mix. Press into the bottom of the springform pan.

3. In the top portion of a double boiler set over medium heat, add in the unsweetened chocolate. Simmer for 3 minutes or until melted. Remove and set aside to cool completely.

4. In a bowl, add in the cream cheese and 1 1/3 cups of white sugar. Beat with an electric mixer until fluffy in consistency. Add in the eggs, 1 cup of sour cream and all-purpose flour. Continue to beat until mixed. Add in the espresso and chocolate mix. Continue to beat until mixed.

5. Pour the filling over the crust.

6. Place into the oven to bake for 1 hour and 10 minutes or until the center is set. Turn off the oven. Allow the cheesecake to rest in the oven for 25 minutes.

7. In a bowl, add in 1 ½ cups of sour cream, 3 tablespoons of white sugar and 1 teaspoon of powdered espresso. Stir well to mix. Spread over the top of the cheesecake. Allow the cheesecake to rest inside of the oven for an additional 5 minutes.

8. Remove the cheesecake from the oven. Remove the cheesecake from the pan and set aside to cool completely. Cover and set into the fridge to chill for 8 hours.

9. Sprinkle the powdered cocoa over the cheesecake.

10. Slice and serve.

Chocolate Fudge Cheesecake

This is a delicious cheesecake dish that every chocoholic will love. It is made with a rich chocolatey glaze and a chocolatey brownie base you will want to spoil yourself with.

Makes: 16 servings

Total Prep Time: 9 hours and 45 minutes

Ingredients:

- ½ cup of pecans, toasted and chopped
- 4, 1 ounce chocolate squares
- 1 cup of butter, soft
- 2 cups of white sugar
- 4 eggs
- 1 cup of all-purpose flour
- 1 tsp. of pure vanilla
- 1 cup of semisweet chocolate pieces
- 4, 8 ounce packs of cream cheese, soft
- 1 ¾ cups of white sugar
- 7 eggs
- 2 tsp. of pure vanilla
- Strawberries, thinly sliced and for garnish

Ingredients for the glaze:

- 1, 12 ounce pack of semisweet chocolate pieces
- ½ cup of heavy whipping cream

Directions:

1. Sprinkle ½ cup of the chopped pecans into the bottom of a greased 9 inch springform pan.

2. In a bowl, add in the chocolate squares. Microwave for 30 seconds or until melted. Stir well until smooth in consistency.

3. In a separate bowl, add in the 1 cup of butter and 2 cups of white sugar. Beat with an electric mixer until smooth in consistency. Add in the 4 eggs and melted chocolate. Continue to beat until fluffy in consistency.

4. Add in the all-purpose flour, pure vanilla and chocolate morsels. Beat on the lowest sett until mixed.

5. Pour the filling over the crust.

6. In a separate bowl, add in the cream cheese. Beat with an electric mixer until smooth in consistency. Add in 1 ¾ cups of white sugar, 7 eggs and 2 teaspoons of pure vanilla. Continue to beat until smooth in consistency. Pour over the brownie batter.

7. Place into the oven to bake for 1 hour and 15 minutes at 325 degrees. Remove and set aside to cool completely. Cover and set into the fridge to chill for 1 hour.

8. Prepare the glaze. In a bowl, add in the chocolate morsels. Melt in the microwave for 1 minute or until smooth in consistency. Add in the heavy whipping cream. Whisk until smooth in consistency. Spread over the top of the cheesecake.

9. Continue to chill the cheesecake for 8 hours.

10. Slice and serve.

Classic Ricotta Cheesecake

This is a simple yet decadent cheesecake that is perfect to make for practically any occasion. It is easy to make and can be ready in just a few hours.

Makes: 12 servings

Total Prep Time: 4 hours and 10 minutes

Ingredients:

- 1 2/3 cups of zwieback crumbs
- 3 Tbsp. of white sugar
- ½ tsp. of powdered cinnamon
- 1/3 cup of butter, soft

Ingredients for the filling:

- 2, 15 ounce cartons of ricotta cheese
- 1 ½ cup of white sugar
- ½ cup of half-and-half
- 2 Tbsp. of all-purpose flour
- 1 Tbsp. of lemon juice
- 1 tsp. of lemon zest
- ¼ tsp. of salt
- 2 eggs, beaten

Ingredients for topping:

- 1 cup of sour cream
- 2 Tbsp. of white sugar
- 1 tsp. of pure vanilla

Directions:

1. In a bowl, add in the zwieback crumbs, white sugar and powdered cinnamon. Add in the butter and stir well to mix until crumbly in consistency. Press into the bottom of a 9 inch springform pan. Cover and place into the fridge to chill until ready for use.

2. Preheat the oven to 350 degrees.

3. In a bowl, add in the ricotta cheese, white sugar, half and half, all-purpose flour, lemon juice, lemon zest, dash of salt and eggs. Beat with an electric mixer until smooth in consistency. Pour over the crust.

4. Transfer the pan onto a baking sheet.

5. Place into the oven to bake for 50 minutes or until the center is set. Remove from the oven and set aside to rest for 15 minutes.

6. In a bowl, add in the sour cream, white sugar and pure vanilla. Beat with an electric mixer until smooth in consistency. Spread carefully over the filling.

7. Place back into the oven to bake for an additional 10 minutes.

8. Remove the cheesecake from the pan. Cover and chill in the fridge for 3 hours.

9. Slice and serve.

Chocolate and Raspberry Cheesecake

This is the perfect cheesecake recipe to prepare for Valentine's day. Each bite is silky smooth and will practically melt in your mouth.

Makes: 12 servings

Total Prep Time: 3 hours and 25 minutes

Ingredients:

- ¾ cup of graham cracker crumbs
- 2 Tbsp. of butter, melted
- 1 envelope of unflavored gelatin
- 1 cup of cold water
- 4 ounces of semisweet chocolate, chopped
- 4, 8 ounce packs of cream cheese, soft
- 1 cup of sugar substitute
- ½ cup of white sugar
- ¼ cup of powdered cocoa
- 2 tsp. of pure vanilla
- 2 cups of raspberries, for topping

Directions:

1. In a bowl, add in the graham cracker crumbs and butter. Stir well to mix. Press into the bottom of a 9 inch springform pan.

2. Place the crust into the oven to bake for 8 to 10 minutes at 375 degrees or until browned. Remove and set aside to cool completely.

3. In a saucepan set over low heat, add in the gelatin and water. Allow to rest for 1 minute or until the gelatin dissolves. Cook for 1 minute. Add in the chopped chocolate and stir well until melted. Remove from heat and set aside to cool.

4. In a bowl, add in the cream cheese, sugar substitute and white sugar. Beat with an electric mixer until smooth in consistency. Add in the chocolate mix and powdered cocoa. Add in the pure vanilla and beat well to incorporate.

5. Pour the filling over the baked crust.

6. Cover and set into the fridge to chill for 3 hours or until firm.

7. Add the raspberries over the top for decoration.

8. Slice and serve.

Conclusion

Well, there you have it!

Hopefully by the end of this cookbook, you have found plenty of cheesecake recipes that you can make for practically any occasion. By the end of this cookbook, not only do I hope you have gained the confidence to make your very own cheesecake from scratch, but have found over 25 delicious cheesecake recipes that will help you to do just that.

So, what is next for you?

The next step for you to take is to begin making all of these delicious cheesecake recipes you have found in this book. Once you have done that, all that is left for you to do is to take what you learned from this book and continue to make any kind of cheesecake recipe you can find.

Good luck!

Author's Afterthoughts

Thanks Ever So Much to Each of My Cherished Readers for Investing the Time to Read This Book!

I know you could have picked from many other books but you chose this one. So, big thanks for buying this book and reading all the way to the end.

If you enjoyed this book or received value from it, I'd like to ask you for a favor. Please take a few minutes to post an honest and heartfelt review on **Amazon.** Your support does make a difference and helps to benefit other people.

Thank you!

Carla Hale

About the Author

Carla Hale

I think of myself as a foodie. I like to eat, yes. I like to cook even more. I like to prepare meals for my family and friends, I feel like that's what I was born to do…

My name is Carla Hale and as may have suspected already, I am originally from Scotland. I am first and foremost a mother, a wife, but simultaneously over the years I became a proclaimed cook. I have shared my recipes with many and will continue to do so, as long as I can. I like different. I dress different, I love different, I speak different and I cook different. I like to think that I am different because I am more animated about what I do than most; I feel more and care more.

It served me right when cooking to sprinkle some tenderness, love, passion, in every dish I prepare. It does not matter if I am preparing a meal for strangers passing by my cooking booth at the flea market or if I am making my mother's favorite recipe. Each and every meal I prepare from scratch will contain a little bite of my life story and little part of my heart in it. People feel it, taste it and ask for more! Thank you for taking the time to get to know me and hopefully through my recipes you can learn a lot more about my influences and preferences. Who knows you might just find your own favorite within my repertoire! Enjoy!

Printed in Great Britain
by Amazon

35690532R00057